How to End a Friendship Nicely

An Approach For Highly Sensitive People

Cara Menae Miller

ISBN: 9781672089838

Names, identifying details, and some circumstantial details in the stories in this book were changed to preserve the anonymity of the individuals involved.

The thoughts I express in this book are my own and may not necessarily reflect the thoughts and experiences of other highly sensitive people.

CONTENTS

ACKNOWLEDGMENTS

I thank Mindy, Celeste, Joe, Patrick, and Sam for making insightful suggestions that improved my book. I thank my writing group for supporting me and encouraging me when I most needed it through the writing and rewriting of this book.

1. CAN YOU END A FRIENDSHIP NICELY?

I chose a somewhat ironic title for my book, "How to End a Friendship Nicely." Obviously, it never feels nice to end a friendship, no matter how you do it. And it won't ever be a "nice" experience for your friend on the receiving end.

Yet, search Google about how to end a friendship. From some of the phrases that generate, you'll see that we are asking Google how to do it nicely, politely, gracefully, and without hurting feelings. Impossible as it seems, we still want to know if there's a way.

I think what we want to know is, how do we end a friendship in a way that is considerate and causes the least amount of pain and stress? But that would make for a very long book title.

I have ended two good friendships in the last few years. In addition, I have had other friendships not work out. In these latter cases, no one needed to "end" anything; we mutually walked or drifted away from each other.

But my book is not about such mutual situations. It is about leaving a friendship when your friend still wants to be friends. Having done this twice, I know so well the overwhelming alarm, confusion, guilt, and grief that goes along with such a heart-wrenching decision. As a highly sensitive person (HSP)[i] with heightened emotions and deep attunement to others, ending each friendship felt to me like performing an unwanted and unexpected violent heart surgery on another person. As if that weren't bad enough, there was no way I could fix the aftermath of hurt and anger in my friend's life.

I feel guilty writing about this topic because I would prefer that none of us ever needed to end a friendship. But here we are, faced with very painful and sometimes unexpected realities. So I tackle this troubling subject in hopes of creating more understanding about it.

In my book, I will share with you my insights on how you know you need to end a friendship. I'll provide you with a list of negative traits that you may recognize in your friend. I will show you signs to look for in your friend that indicate you won't be able to work things out. I will then provide you with a communication approach you can use to end your friendship. Finally, I will help you navigate the aftermath of ending your friendship.

Airplanes

I think a friendship can be compared to a pair of airplanes, which is why I chose them for my book cover. Healthy friends fly alongside each other because they enjoy traveling through life together. Both friends respect each other's boundaries and limits and can freely be themselves.

But if your friend demonstrates an inability to respect your boundaries and limits and true self, then you must suppress everything your friend doesn't like, so you can keep flying alongside each other smoothly. *Or*, you must be honest and create "turbulence."

I think it is far better to be yourself and create this "turbulence" with your friend at your first available opportunities. This "turbulence" will cause your friend to "steer" away from you before you get any deeper into the friendship.

After all, your friend won't find it pleasant to "fly" alongside you if it's not a smooth ride. In my friendships that didn't work out, my biggest regret is failing to be true to myself from day one.

Since you picked up my book, I assume you relate to my regret. It's too late for you to go back in time and go about your friendship differently. You are already deep into a friendship that you now want to leave, and you don't know how to get out.

I've been there. I know your overwhelming stress and pain, and in the rest of my book I'd like to help you make the smoothest possible exit. Dare I say, I'd like to help you end your friendship nicely.

Throughout my book, I often use the singular noun "friend" followed by plural pronouns like "they" and "their" in the same sentence in order to be inclusive of all genders.

2. FREEDOM

"Think for a while of all the coercion and control that you submit to on the part of others when you so anxiously live up to their expectations in order to buy their love and approval or because you fear you will lose them. Each time you submit to this control and this coercion you destroy the capacity to love which is your very nature, for you cannot but do to others what you allow others to do to you. Contemplate, then, all the control and coercion in your life and hopefully this contemplation alone will cause them to drop. The moment they drop, freedom will arise. And freedom is just another word for love."

-Anthony De Mello[ii]

My friendship-ending experiences have taught me that freedom is *very* important in relationships. I must be free to set boundaries. I must be free to express limits. I must be free to be honest and to be myself. If a friend doesn't allow me these freedoms, the friendship is strained. My mental health suffers, and I resent my friend.

I am not suggesting our friends must be perfect. All of us have faults, blind spots, and weaknesses. We have bad days, and we have different opinions. It's okay for us to be accommodating of each other's weaknesses and differences to an extent. But if your friendship doesn't have room for your true self, then you are not really free; you're trapped. And that takes away your ability to love, since love must be free.

So, how do you know when you are not free in a friendship?

You just *know*. But here are some signs you can look for:

- You don't feel free to be honest with your friend.
- You don't feel free to stand up to your friend.
- You friend doesn't like the word, "No."
- You feel like you're walking on eggshells around your friend.
- Your friend doesn't want to be challenged or disagreed with.
- Your friend would be very upset if you needed space or ended the friendship.
- Your friendship requires more than you can give.
- You feel obligated to spend time with your friend.
- You find yourself contacting your friend even when you don't want to.
- Your friendship is eroding your happiness and inner peace.

- Your friendship is adding significant stress to your life.
- Anger and resentment toward your friend are building up.
- You have a lot of negative thoughts about your friend.
- You daydream about not being in this friendship anymore.
- You regret becoming close with your friend.
- You're wondering how to exit the friendship.

If you feel this way, there are reasons. Your friend has some negative traits that are making you want to leave, and we'll look at them in the next chapter.

The last five years have taught me more about friendship than all the years that came before. These hard lessons began in 2015. It was a particularly rough year for me, friendship wise.

That year, some of my friendships didn't work out. I talked with each one, hoping to give each friendship a chance. But our differences could not be reconciled.

The first situation involved Melissa and Kate. The three of us started getting together every Saturday night for dinner. We opened up about what was going on in our lives and what we were learning from our relationships. But I had no idea what was coming.

Melissa got into some arguments with her coworker, Jim, who was also a mutual friend of ours. Jim rubbed Melissa the wrong way and reminded her of someone from her past, so she tried to get him fired. That didn't work, so she hired a private investigator to search his records. The investigator didn't find anything that Melissa could use against him. During this upheaval, Kate sided with Melissa. The two of them began talking badly about Jim to other people we knew.

Ultimately, I let Melissa and Kate know that I didn't think their contention with Jim was necessary. But they didn't budge. Then I learned they were talking about me behind my back. I bowed out of Saturday night dinners, worn out from the stress and tension.

That same year I roomed with a girl named Anna whose boyfriend of two years broke up with her. Before the breakup, she would say, "There is no one better than Sam." But after they broke up, she spent hours telling anyone who would listen about Sam's numerous character flaws. Our other roommates rushed to Anna's side. Yet all this did was encourage her to keep venting. Her venting degenerated into loud yelling and cussing as well as tantrums on the floor. Her criticism wasn't limited to Sam. She found things wrong with other people, cutting down their looks and "seeing" personality and character flaws in them that were not necessarily there.

Anna and I had three big conversations. In each one, I let her know I needed more peace and quiet in our home, and I explained that her critical statements of others were unfair. Anna responded defensively each time, yet with some promise to change. Nonetheless, her cutting remarks continued, and I moved out after 14 months.

Because of my honesty with Melissa, Kate, and Anna, my friendships with them did not work out. Then, in the last few years, I had to walk away from two more friends: Leslie and Natasha. I'll tell you about them later on.

As you can imagine, I have learned a lot about negative traits I need to look out for when I'm making new friends. I can now spot these traits from miles away and avoid close friendships with those who show them. I have compiled these traits into a list I call "The Friend Who" List. Let's take a look at it in the next chapter.

3. "THE FRIEND WHO..."

Below is a list of traits that may make you want to leave a friendship. I call it "The Friend Who" List. *All* of us can be guilty of these traits sometimes, so it's important for us to forgive and help each other when we falter. But if the trait is ongoing and shows no sign of budging, then the impact becomes too negative. Bad friend traits can come in clusters, and I've had friends who show several of these traits simultaneously.

I don't know your friendship situation. But can you recognize your friend's trait(s) on this list?

"The Friend Who" List

Needy

The friend who too often needs more than you can give, whether it's free babysitting, free paper editing, favors, money, emotional therapy, or just too much of your time and attention.

Reactive

The friend who is unstable to the point of mistreating you. This friend may be insecure, defensive, and unhappy and therefore reacts to you by lashing out at you even when you've said and done nothing wrong.

Offended

The friend who you can't challenge, disagree with, or share an alternative perspective with unless you want backlash. If you disagree with this friend, they'll seek a second opinion until they find one they want to hear.

Competing

The friend who competes with you when it comes to love interests, social status, success, or even material things like clothing, cars, and accessories. This friend feels the need to be ahead and to one-up you.

Plan-Ditching

The friend who ditches plans with you regularly for any reason—something better came up, their love interest became available, or they just don't feel like getting together.

Bad Decision-Making

The friend who makes the same poor decisions again and again, despite your warnings and advice, yet keeps coming back for your listening ear, your unconditional understanding, and your help with picking up the pieces.

Converting

The friend who is trying to convert you to their political group, religion, diet, or something else.

Even when you've said, "No," their agenda remains. They can't seem to drop it.

Friends with Benefits

The friend who isn't exactly just a friend. The benefits may be physical or just emotional. One of you doesn't want to move forward into a romantic relationship, but both of you can't seem to stop benefitting.

Complaining

The friend who is constantly complaining about other people. This friend may be emotionally troubled, defensive, angry, or have a sense of entitlement. Regardless of the reason, complaining is at the forefront of their conversations.

Blabbering

The friend who blabs about anyone and everyone behind their backs, telling you their personal problems and even divulging the skeletons in their closet, all the time knowing those "secrets" were supposed to be kept confidential.

Projecting

The friend who lacks self-awareness and projects their issues onto you. This friend dresses frumpily but tells you to dress better. This friend had a rough childhood but keeps psychoanalyzing *you*. This friend is angry but tells you to work on *your* anger.

Judging

The friend who is preoccupied with judging you. This is the friend who can't seem to see you in a positive light or be happy for you. Their judgement of you is unwarranted, exaggerated, or a result of their own projection.

Narcissistic

The friend who doesn't care about you. You are only in their life for what you can do or be for them. Any words or actions that look like "caring" are selfishly motivated. This friend does just what is necessary to keep you in their life for their own benefit.

Drastically Changing

The friend who drastically changes their worldview, values, and attitudes but doesn't want your friendship to change. Although your friend's new identity isn't who you are, your friend shouts it from the rooftops and dares you to have a problem with it.

Drama-Starting

The friend who starts conflict and drama everywhere. This friend is suspicious and quick to accuse, leading to unnecessary conflicts. This friend works to recruit others to their "side" and is regularly venting, gossiping, and scheming.

Drama-Supporting

The friend who *supports* the friend who starts conflict and drama everywhere. You thought your friend was cool until you noticed they always side with the Drama-Starter. Your friend has a knack for supporting those with a victim mentality.

Deceiving

The friend who conceals what they really think, feel, or do. Your friend avoids telling the truth or outright deceives you with lies, sugarcoating, or false fronts.

Habit Forming

The friend who is your friend because they want to drink, do drugs, party, or engage in some other activity with you that you don't want in your life anymore. You don't want to enable this friend, and you are also trying to make better decisions for yourself.

The Victim Mentality Cluster

In addition to the "The Friend Who" list of individual traits, you may discover that some of your friends show a "cluster" of traits. I found this to be especially true of friends who exhibit victim mentalities.[iii] Each friendship of mine that didn't work out was due, at least in part, to my friend having a victim mentality. The victim mentality cluster of traits often includes Reactive, Offended, Bad Decision-Making, Complaining, Projecting, Judging, Drama-Starting, and Drama-Supporting.

I absolutely *love* listening to and helping friends and family through hard times. With a background in psychological counseling, it's one of my absolute favorite things to do.

But I've learned the hard way that this is entirely different from enabling and coddling friends with victim mentalities. The longer you listen to them, the more you notice they are always focused on the bad or negative things that keep "happening" to them, and they therefore complain a lot. They tend to be angry and resentful about things not going their way. They don't see themselves as responsible; forces and people outside them are always to blame for their problems and feelings. They show little interest and effort in making personal changes. The longer you try to help them, the more you see there is no end in sight, because they don't see the role they play in their problems and perspectives.

I completely understand how easy it is to fall into a victim mentality when things are going badly. I am not saying that falling into it for a few hours or a few days is a deal breaker in a friendship. But when friends are entrenched in the victim mentality, they can't be healthy friends.

People with victim mentalities attract friends who *support* victim mentalities. I have noticed this with Drama-Starters and Drama-Supporters. Drama-Supporters are always rushing to the side of any person playing the victim, providing support and agreement for every one of their complaints and conflicts. Drama-Supporters never side with the healthier people who are calling out the drama. Therefore, whenever you walk away from a Drama-Starter, you often have to leave the Drama-Supporters behind, too.

What About Your Friend?

Of course, the victim mentality is not the only downfall in friendships—there are many others. "The Friend Who" List shows just how many traits, either alone or in clusters, can cause the demise of a friendship.

Did you recognize your friend when you read through the list? Even if you did, I encourage you to come up with your own unique sentence that begins with, "The Friend Who..." Clarify for yourself why your friendship is bothering you. That will help you as you continue the rest of this journey.

In the next chapter, I want to share with you some of my deeper observations about why your friendship is bothering you.

4. CROSSING, STRETCHING, AND SLICING

As I mentioned earlier, I had to end two good friendships in the last few years. The first one was with a girl named Leslie.

Leslie and I were best friends for 12 years when she joined a religious-political movement. She devoured their blogs, podcasts, and books. She attended their gatherings. Under the influence of the movement, her religion and politics changed drastically from what they once were. I listened to and read the podcasts and books she suggested, but I couldn't jump on her bandwagon.

Our friendship may have survived if her views had been the only thing that changed. But the deeper problem was that her attitude and personality also changed. She became antagonistic toward those outside her newfound movement.

She complained to me about her family and friends because she now disagreed with their beliefs. She began having more problems in her relationships. She had angry outbursts, even swearing at people who angered her, something she wouldn't have done in the past. She seemed to have regressed to a teenage angst, even though she was in her late 30s. I didn't recognize her anymore.

This movement was all she could talk about, and our conversations were wearing me down. A few times, I challenged some of her statements and pointed out some of her unfair stereotypes.

But anything I told her went in one ear and out the other, and she would change the subject when we didn't agree. Our friendship was not at all what it used to be, and I was drained.

Leslie wanted our friendship to remain the same even though her attitude and personality had done a 180-degree turn. I finally got to a breaking point when nothing in me wanted to spend any more time with her.

As for what happened to my friendship with Leslie, stay tuned.

The Big Picture

I like to see the big picture. So, I boiled down the negative traits on "The Friend Who" list into three broad categories: Crossing, Stretching, and Slicing. This sounds like cutting vegetables while doing yoga on a busy highway, but that's not it. What I mean is, your friend is doing one or more of these three things:

- **Crossing** your boundaries
- **Stretching** your limits
- Wanting only a **Slice** of your friendship

When a friendship hasn't worked out, it was for one of these three reasons. I'll explain each of them.

Crossing

I've had friends who crossed my boundaries. They made hurtful comments that were the result of their own projection; they would insult me about the very things in their lives they were most unhappy about. In addition, they were not good at taking no for an answer. They disregarded my "No" or tried to turn my "No" into a "Yes" using manipulation. Lastly, they persisted in disregarding the same boundaries I had already set with them. During the times I had not set explicit boundaries, they disrespected what they knew to be my preferences and opinions. Friends who cross boundaries may have some of the following traits from "The Friend Who" list: Needy, Reactive, Offended, Converting, Blabbering, Projecting, Judging, and Deceiving. Crossing boundaries is always a sign of disrespect.

Some people seem to think we "set" boundaries in order for them to be crossed, as if our hope is to "catch" them and challenge them if they stray over the line. That's not usually the case. Rather, healthy people almost always perceive boundaries implicitly, without having to be told. They know instinctively not to insult others, not to take their own frustrations out on others, and to respect when someone says, "No." Do you really want to spend time with someone you have to set boundaries with right and left? That's a relationship that likely won't end well.

Stretching

I've had friends who stretched my limits. They wanted more time, help, favors, energy, patience, or understanding than I could give. Friends who stretch limits may have some of the following traits from "The Friend Who" list: Needy, Plan-Ditching, Bad Decision-Making, Friends with Benefits, Drastically Changing, Drama-Starting, and Drama-Supporting, although any trait on the list can stretch limits.

Your limits are overly stretched when there is some resource your friend wants to draw from you that you don't have more of to give, and that resource can be anything at all, internal or external.

In such scenarios, I felt my limits stretching like a worn rubber band. Right when I thought, *"I can do this!"* the rubber band would break.

I thought I could provide a friend with frequent, ongoing emotional therapy.

I thought I could listen... and listen... and listen... to a friend whose perspective I didn't agree with.

I thought I could keep giving someone a chance who kept canceling plans.

I thought I could offer "help" to someone who kept sabotaging their own life.

I thought I could continue to be close friends when we weren't on the same page.

I thought I could keep the same friendship with someone who had drastically changed.

I thought I could provide unconditional positive regard to someone with a victim mentality.

I ignored what my limits were trying to tell me, over and over again. Eventually, I'd psychologically implode. I'd become very irritable, have difficulty sleeping, or find myself fretting around the clock. I would then have to acknowledge my limits because my mind and body forced me to.

I now listen to my limits the first time they speak up.

If you are like me—ultra conscientious, compassionate, and wishing you could save people—then it's easy to feel guilty about limits. I have some helping-gone-wrong stories where I tried to give much more than I could. I started out believing I could be everything someone wanted or needed me to be. In the end, I fell flat on my face, my limits crashing around me.

I've learned that our limits make us finite and human. They keep us humble. They help us see that there are fences and property lines around what is our responsibility and what is not; what we are capable of and what we are not.

But the very best thing about our limits is that *we* decide what they are. No one else gets to.

Slicing

Lastly, I've had friends who "sliced" our friendship. What I mean is, these friends didn't want my whole self but only the slice of me that was to their liking: a constant listening ear, agreement with everything they said, or favors. Friends who "slice" friendships may have some of the following traits from the "The Friend Who" list: Needy, Reactive, Offended, Converting, Friends with Benefits, Narcissistic, Drastically Changing, and Habit Forming. These types of friends want *something* from you, but that something is never *all* of you.

But your whole self is all you can be in the long run. If you pretend to be just a "slice" of yourself, the truth will come out eventually. Then you will both see that you were living the lie your friend wanted you to live.

Friends who are "slicing" your friendship want the slice of you that sets no boundaries or limits. They want the slice of you that always agrees with them. They want the slice of you that fits their agenda. They want the slice of you that can do or be something for them. These relationships tend to be imbalanced and unfair. Friends who "slice" your friendship are allowed to say whatever they want, but they censor *you*. Or they can behave however they want but expect you to behave to their liking. Or their needs are at the center of your friendship, while yours are disregarded. You exist to make them feel good or to make some part of their lives better. You feel like they've drawn a box around you and have you right where they want you. If you step outside those lines, you know their reaction won't be pretty.

Talk about feeling trapped! The friend who is "slicing" your friendship certainly doesn't allow you the freedom that healthy friendships should.

Is your friend crossing your boundaries, stretching your limits, and/or slicing your friendship? Keep in mind that Crossing, Stretching, and Slicing can overlap; you may have a friend who is doing more than one of these or even all three. Consider writing a paragraph describing the ways your friend is doing one or more of these things. This clarity will help motivate you to walk away.

5. ENDING A FRIENDSHIP USING S-S-P

When your friend doesn't allow you to be your true self, you will get to a breaking point. Even if you have decided that you can "do this"—that you can "handle" this friendship—your body will tell you otherwise. You'll feel too stressed and angry to function well. You may start taking your frustrations out on other people. You may overeat or undereat. You may sleep more or sleep less. You may have other psychological and physical symptoms. You may become almost incapable of pretending with your friend anymore.

It is ideal to recognize an unhealthy friendship and end it before reaching this breaking point. But if you are like me, the breaking point sometimes must occur before you finally get that a friendship isn't good for you.

Should I Try to Work Things Out With My Friend?

At the point of crisis, you may wonder, "Should I try to work things out with my friend before leaving the friendship?"

This question has its own heading because I've wrestled hard with it. I've endured an enormous amount of guilt for not trying harder to work things out with the two friends I left behind. Yet I had solid reasons for not trying harder, and in the end those reasons won.

The reasons were simple. I knew the friendships could not work out because our differences were irreconcilable. So why subject myself to messy conversations that would result in unnecessary pain and stress for both of us? I did not want to give these friends yet more opportunities to mistreat me or manipulate me. I didn't want them to try to talk me out of my decision. I did not want to give them any more chances to disregard my boundaries, limits, and opinions. They'd already done those things, which was why I wanted to leave.

When a friendship is unhealthy, trying to work things out will not help. You can give it a chance to change, or not give it a chance to change. Either way, the result is the same: the friendship won't change. Unfortunately, I learned this the hard way several times before finally getting it. I used to think that if I showed unconditional acceptance and compassion for difficult friends, they'd someday start treating me well (false).

Then I thought that if I did the "mature thing" by talking respectfully to them about the problems in the friendship, things would turn around (also false). The truth is, it doesn't matter what you say or how you say it to an unhealthy friend—you will still get an unhealthy response.

To make this more concrete, here are signs that you have a friend you won't be able to work things out with:

- Your friend has traits from "The Friend Who" list that are ingrained and show no signs of budging.
- Your friend has difficulty with other friends—not just you—because of these traits.
- Others have confronted your friend and have not had success in working things out.

- Your friend has failed to show respect for (or tried to talk you out of) your boundaries, limits, and differences.
- Your feel manipulated by your friend.
- Your friend gets defiant and defensive when challenged or disagreed with.
- Your friend does not sincerely apologize when confronted. Any "apology" is sandwiched between defensiveness, denial, and rationalizations.
- Your friend plays the victim when confronted.
- Your friend crosses yet more lines when confronted.
- Your friend expresses no interest in changing.
- Your friend sometimes expresses interest in changing but doesn't follow through.
- Your friend sees the source of their problems outside them but never within them.

- Your friend finds fault in others but not in themselves.
- Your friend has an anger problem.
- Your friend has a victim mentality.
- Your friend may be self-deprecating, but this self-deprecation does not lead to a sincere desire to own their mistakes and change.

If your friend is showing any of these signs, don't feel bad for ending the friendship without trying harder to salvage it. You have a right to leave a friendship if it's not healthy for you, if your friend is showing signs of not being willing to change, or if you have no more desire to be in the friendship.

S-S-P

Yet trying to figure out "how" to leave a friendship can be confusing and overwhelming and cause a great deal of stress. Sometimes there isn't even much time to figure out what to do. If your friend is texting you, calling you, or expecting to get together with you soon, then you may need to decide what to do "on the fly."

That was my situation with Leslie. I only had a couple of days before she expected us to talk on the phone to "catch up." That gave me 48 hours to figure out how to break it to Leslie that I didn't want to be friends anymore. It was an incredibly stressful 48 hours, to put it mildly.

I will share with you the communication method I used. It was based on my mom's advice and was what I felt I could manage in the midst of my overwhelmed nerves. Only *after* I communicated in this way did I figure out what I did. Using email, I shared with Leslie what I was experiencing and why I was experiencing it, and I canceled our upcoming plans. I later named this communication approach S-S-P.

S-S-P stands for Share, Specific, and Present. It involves **S**haring your experience about **S**pecific issues in your friendship along with a **P**resent-time decision to create immediate distance. The intention is not to work things out but rather to leave the friendship.

S-S-P can absolutely be expressed in your own words. It can be short or long and expressed in any order. S-S-P can be communicated over the phone, in a handwritten letter, in an email, or via text—any communication that feels comfortable for you. It's far better to communicate than to ghost without any communication. I personally felt best communicating S-S-P in an email, though I think a handwritten letter is a great idea as well.

You may communicate S-S-P to your friend in person. But consider the risks. The conversation could take a stressful turn if your friend gets upset by the encounter and lashes out, becomes accusatory, or tries to talk you out of your perspective on the spot. You risk backing down from your decision, saying things you will later regret, or having yet another upsetting encounter with this friend. But if you are not concerned about these risks and feel better about meeting in person, you can.

Examples of S-S-P will be included in Chapter 6. For now, let's look at what it is.

Share

Share what you are feeling and experiencing in your friendship that's negative. When possible, look for feelings other than just anger. This is where you share that you are feeling stressed, sad, frustrated, confused, surprised, drained, at a breaking point, at a crossroads, unable to be yourself, or *whatever* it is that you are feeling and experiencing.

Specific

What **specific**ally about your friendship led to your negative experience? Being specific does not mean being accusatory and emotionally charged; it's best to remain factual and neutral. This is where you state what boundaries your friend has been crossing, which of your limits are overly stretched, or what ways you have not been able to be yourself. You don't have to give *every* example that has occurred or even list every single issue; your friend is smart enough to recall the details of your friendship. Just say enough to ensure your friend understands the general problems and isn't left in the dark.

Both sharing your feelings and being specific about the issue will keep your friend from wracking their brain for months or years, trying to figure out what they did wrong.

Now we get to the "P" in S-S-P, which is what you can say to end your friendship.

Present

Tell your friend what you need to do in the **present** time to create immediate distance from the friendship. Your present-time decision can be any statement that stops you from seeing your friend in the foreseeable future. That can be canceling plans, bowing out of the weekly activity you do together, or saying you don't want to get together at this time. Your creativity is your only limit. The point is that you stay rooted in your present need to stop spending time with your friend. Your hope is that your friend will then "steer" away from you without you having to say anything more.

Of course, there is nothing wrong with being more direct and telling your friend that the friendship is over. Some people would consider this the best thing to do. If you have the courage and desire to do so, then communicate that you don't want to continue the friendship.

Yet many people can't bring themselves to say that. Speaking for myself, all I could manage with Leslie and Natasha was to state a present-time decision. I felt utterly overwhelmed and even paralyzed at the prospect of telling them that the friendship was over.

Whether you are highly sensitive like me or not, stating a present-time decision could be wise for a few reasons.

First, there is nothing more real than the present moment. The past and the future do not exist, so you are justified in staying rooted in what you need in the present. Secondly, a present-time decision is probably all you need to state to let go of a friendship. Your friend is not likely to pursue you afterwards. Thirdly, stating a present-time decision is less overwhelming than saying that the relationship is over. Therefore, you are more likely to have the courage to go through with it. This keeps you from doing the disappearing act by ghosting your friend.

Now that you understand more about each part of S-S-P, I'll share in the next chapter how I used it to walk away from Leslie and Natasha. Then I'll offer ideas for each part of S-S-P that will get your mind thinking creatively as you form your own S-S-P message.

6. S-S-P EXAMPLES

Recall that I was best friends with Leslie for many years until she joined a religious-political movement and underwent a 180-degree personality change. The end of our friendship came about when Leslie asked if we could talk on the phone on an upcoming weekend.

My text message response was, *"Sure!"*

But I was uneasy. I imagined another strained phone conversation listening to Leslie vent, and nothing in me had the energy for it. My body was screaming, *"No."*

I paced around my house wondering how I was going to get out of the upcoming phone call, let alone our long-held friendship. Then I did what I usually do when I'm fretting: I called my mom.

My mom guided me to email Leslie and to make the email about me as much as I could, avoiding critical statements about Leslie or the movement she had joined. She suggested I focus on the sadness that was behind my annoyance and anger. With her guidance, I came up with the following email:

Dear Leslie,

I haven't been feeling the energy over the last few weeks for our conversations. I have realized that I am sad about the path you have taken. It's not who I am, and it is very different than who you once were. I am grieving that the strong connection we used to have is gone.

I truly hoped to understand this movement and perhaps even join it alongside you. Yet after learning more about it, I am unable to. It's not who I am. I am unsure what to say during our conversations, and I don't feel like I can be myself anymore in our friendship.

Because of how I am feeling, I'd rather not catch up right now. I hope you can understand.

Love, Cara

I pushed "Send" with a lot of trepidation yet, strangely, with a sense of peace. I felt like I'd said just the right things and nothing more.

I later realized why I felt good about the email and was able to identify S-S-P as the approach I had used. As for how Leslie responded, I will let you know in the final chapter.

Months after I ended my friendship with Leslie,

I reached out to a girl named Natasha who was going through a very hard time. Unfortunately, Natasha became the second friend I needed to walk away from.

During the year and a half of my friendship with Natasha, she made cutting remarks about my looks, including my weight and my clothing choices. She lashed out when she didn't get her way or when I said anything she didn't agree with. She crossed boundaries I had set. She complained constantly about her life and the people in it. She insulted our mutual friends behind their backs anytime they didn't give her what she wanted or say what she wanted to hear.

I excused her behavior for quite a while because she was going through "a very difficult time." I kept hoping it was just a phase and that she would come out of it. Then, at the year-and-a-half mark of our friendship, I became overstressed and was sleeping less than usual. I found myself experiencing every single sign, listed in chapter two, that I wasn't free in my friendship with Natasha. I came to the dreadful realization that her friendship was not merely difficult; it was unhealthy for me and could not continue.

When she next texted me to get together, I replied via text that I was feeling stressed and that our friendship was taking a toll on my mental health (Share). I said I was unable to hear more complaints from her about our friends (Specific). I also said that her negativity about dating and relationships was more than I could handle any longer (Specific). I told her I would not be able to get together and that I needed a lot of space (Present-time decision).

Natasha sent me a few text messages back. Although she did say, "I'm sorry," her apology was sandwiched between defensiveness, rationalizations, denial, and even a couple of "polite" jabs at me. She then requested we talk it out in person.

I decided not to do it. Regardless of how awful I felt about this decision, I still believe it was best. Natasha showed the signs from Chapter 5 that she wouldn't change and, therefore, "talking it out" would be unproductive at best and potentially disastrous. I had already been down the road of "talking it out" with friends who treated me poorly. It never did resolve anything and only created more opportunities for them to manipulate and mistreat me.

So, I responded to Natasha that what I really needed was space.

She replied that she "wished me well." Then, in the following weeks, she included me in a few group-text invitations to her parties. I felt stressed and guilty that my request for space had not registered with her. I replied to her third invitation, asking her to please remove me from the group thread.

She replied with a not-nice message, and at the end of it she said she would not get in touch with me again.

S-S-P can be messy... So, in the last chapter of my book we will look at how you can deal with the potential aftermath of ending a friendship.

But before we do, below are some ideas for each part of S-S-P that could get your creativity flowing. You might also consider reaching out to friends and family who can help you with wording.

"Share" Examples

Here are some ideas for words and phrases you can include when you are sharing your negative feelings or experience:

- Stressed
- Overwhelmed

- Low on energy
- Sad
- Confused
- Frustrated
- Surprised
- Angry
- Feeling the need for a change
- At a breaking point
- Unable to be supportive
- Unable to relate
- Unable to agree
- Unable to give as much as I hoped to
- Unable to help in the way I had hoped
- Feeling like I can't be myself
- Feeling like I need to take better care of myself
- Feeling the need to focus on myself

"Specific" Examples

The specific problems in your friendship may not be able to be captured in general examples, but the following ideas may help. You may have more than one "specific" to share with your friend, which could be a combination of issues and examples.

- We are on two different paths
- Our values are different
- We are not on the same page
- We have grown apart
- I don't feel like we are connecting
- You have been cancelling the plans we make
- Your statements about _____ are not okay with me
- Your statements about _____ are more than I can handle
- It is too difficult for me to trust you to keep the things I share private
- I don't have any interest in competing with you
- I feel a lot of anger coming from you that I don't think is fair to me

- I am hearing a lot of complaining and negativity
- I don't agree with your perspective about...
- I can't be supportive of your decisions about...
- I don't feel like my advice and help is making a difference
- The boundaries I have set have not been respected
- I don't think the issues in our friendship can be resolved

"Present" examples

- I won't be coming to Saturday night dinners anymore
- I won't be able to babysit and housesit for you any longer
- I don't want to talk on the phone right now
- I don't think that getting together at this

time is a good idea for me

- I need to cancel our plans this weekend
- I need a lot of space at this time
- I've decided not to continue participating in our small group
- I don't foresee us hanging out again
- I need to cancel our road trip
- I don't want to make any more plans with you at this time
- I don't want to get together right now

As you are coming up with the right words, think about whether there is Crossing, Stretching, or Slicing going on in your friendship. That will help guide you in what to say—you'll either be sharing more about your boundaries, your limits, or your true self in your message. Maybe you'll be sharing more about all three!

If you are communicating S-S-P to someone you will not be able to avoid—a coworker or fellow church member or someone you share community connections with—then a wise option for "P" could be stating that you want to scale your friendship back. You could say you want to scale your friendship back to an acquaintanceship or simply scale it back to something casual. Your friend will understand from this that you don't want a deep and involved friendship anymore. Wording it this way could make it less awkward when you must be around each other. Perhaps you can still say hello or engage in some casual small talk when you absolutely can't avoid each other.

I hope I was able to get you thinking creatively about words and phrases you can use as you work on your S-S-P communication.

7. QUESTIONS AND STRUGGLES

Did it look like I was leaving you hanging at the end of the last chapter? ;-) Don't worry; I realize there are more questions and struggles you might have about sending your friend an S-S-P message. I had them too!

What If I Don't Have the Courage?

I understand how hard it is, palms sweating and heart pounding, to push the "Send" button with a message to end a friendship. These were some of the most awful moments of my life that I couldn't wait to be over. If you are finding yourself totally paralyzed and unable to communicate S-S-P to your friend, I can relate. What you may need, in this case, is to buy yourself more time and space as you consider what to say to your friend. If this is what you need, you could send something more general when your friend next wants to get together:

I am going to pass on getting together. Right now, I need to pull back and spend some time thinking about our friendship.

Or,

I am going to pass on getting together. Right now, I need to pull back and focus on myself. I'll get back in touch when I'm ready.

Buying yourself extra time and space will give you the chance to calm your nerves. It will also give you more time to talk to friends and family about how to best to word your final message to your friend.

Personally, I find that getting it over with is best. If you feel really good about your S-S-P message, that will also make it easier to press "Send."

Yet another thing that can take the edge off is this: plan to not read any response you get back. Find a friend or family member who will agree to read it for you and give you the general gist of it—only what you need or want to know. That person can then permanently delete the message for you so you never have to lay eyes on it. If you know in advance that someone else will be reading the response for you, this can calm you down enough to press that "Send" button.

What If I Never Stood Up to My Friend?

I am much better at standing up for myself now. But I used to be very poor at it. So I am familiar with the guilt and regret of that failure.

If you never once stood up to your friend, then you could benefit from working out that honesty muscle before leaving the friendship. So the next time you have a conversation with your friend, try being honest about your boundary, your limit, or your true thoughts and opinions. See how your friend responds.

Get this: if you stand up to your friend, the friendship might even end without you needing to leave it with S-S-P. Twice in my life, a friend stopped contacting me simply because I stood up to her! In one situation, all I did was say no to her pressuring me for a favor. I never heard from her again, although up to that point she had made weekly plans with me!

Or you may stand up to your friend and get a disrespectful reaction. Then you will always know that at least you tried being more honest before walking away.

So, since you don't really know how your friend will respond, I encourage you to try standing up for yourself. See how things play out.

Or, you may be 100% sure that this friendship cannot be right or healthy for you and that you don't want it anymore, regardless of the fact that you never stood up for yourself. If this is the case, then your S-S-P *is* your way of standing up for yourself, so see it that way and be proud.

What If My Friend Did Nothing Wrong?

Maybe your friend did nothing wrong and does not have any of the negative traits from "The Friend Who" List. Do you simply feel that you and your friend have grown apart? Or that you just don't have the same interest in being friends that you used to? If so, you may struggle with feeling bad, and you may feel at a loss for what to say.

An S-S-P message can still work well in this situation. The only difference is it won't involve any negative feelings or issues. You can decline to get together and then share what are you are feeling and why.

Maybe you feel unmotivated to get together because you don't feel like you two share the same interests anymore.

Or you don't feel you have anything to give to the friendship because you are focused on other obligations and relationships.

Or you feel that you don't have the time to give to the friendship because you have enough things on your plate.

Whatever it is you are feeling and why, you can include in your message that your decision is not a negative reflection of your friend. This could keep your friend from taking your decision too personally.

What If I'm to blame?

As you know, my biggest regret in friendships is not standing up for myself often enough.

That's not my only regret, though. There are other ways I've handled difficult friendships that I'm not proud of. I have let anger build up far too much because I remained silent for too long about what wasn't okay. Or I gave a friend too many chances after standing up for myself. When my roommate Anna from Chapter 2 crossed the same boundaries that I'd set more than once, I raised my voice at her. I can think of times when I pretended to have sympathy and compassion when what I really felt was the need to challenge a friend. Lastly, I have talked about some of my difficult friends behind their backs more than I needed to. All this is to say, I look back and wish I'd handled these situations better.

However, I no longer feel guilty walking away from unhealthy friendships, and you shouldn't either. If you have made mistakes, it doesn't follow that you should have to stay in the friendship. Unhealthy friendships don't help either person involved, so it is not productive to "punish" yourself by staying in them.

If you feel that you are to blame in some ways, you might be wondering whether to apologize in your S-S-P message. That's a great question, and it depends.

If you are like me and tend to take too much responsibility for problems in friendships, then be careful about apologizing. I have over-apologized in difficult friendships before, and all this did was help my friend keep believing that any problems in our friendship were my fault when they weren't.

If *both* you and your friend were mistreating each other, though, then in your S-S-P message it might be good to mention the unhealthy *dynamic* between you rather than to mention either of you individually.

Will My Friend Retaliate?

Maybe you fear what your friend might say about you behind your back once you leave the friendship. I have had this fear myself, and my fear has come true in some cases—former friends have judged me and talked about me behind my back. Some people's egos are so fragile that they feel the need to bolster it up when it's bruised. This means they feel the need to make you look bad if you walk away from them.

If this is something your friend may do, there's nothing you can do to control that. Take comfort that the people closest to you know you well enough to disregard anything said about you that isn't accurate. The only thing you can do in this situation is word your S-S-P message in a way that you won't regret later. Imagine your friend telling other people what your S-S-P message says. With that in mind, craft your message in a way that expresses yourself authentically and vulnerably.

Maybe you fear that your friend will try to become closer to your mutual friends in order to get on their "good side" or else try to have as much fun as possible with your friends without you there.

But no matter what your friend might do or say, decide to follow through with your decision to leave the friendship. Don't be intimidated into staying in it. Don't feel the need to do any damage control either now or later. Just keep doing what you're doing. Keep your peace.

In the last chapter, I will aim to help you deal with the struggles you may have *after* you send your message.

8. THE AFTERMATH

As promised, I'll tell you how Leslie responded to my S-S-P message. She wrote a very long email reply with a lot of cussing and accusations, tearing down everything about me she could think of. The nicest thing she said to me in her email was that I am a horrible person.

And, as you recall from the previous chapter, Natasha's response to my S-S-P text message was a bit messy.

We now cycle back to what I said in Chapter 1: it never feels nice to end a friendship, no matter how you do it. And it won't be a "nice" experience for your friend on the receiving end. Yet I have suggested how you might end a friendship "nicely" using S-S-P. Communicating with S-S-P avoids ghosting, but also avoids the unnecessary pain and stress that could come with a formal "breakup" talk.

Still, don't expect to feel good after you send your message, and don't expect your friend to appreciate it. This chapter is about navigating the aftermath of ending a friendship. I want to prepare you for what you may encounter.

Your Friend's Response

Your friend may not respond to your S-S-P communication. Your friend may be too hurt or not want to converse about your decision to leave the friendship. Or, your friend may respond with anger, defensiveness, and accusations, as Leslie did. Honestly, those two possibilities are the easiest for you, because you will not feel tempted to get back in touch with your friend. It's over.

But the third possibility is stickier: your friend may not let you go easily. Your friend may be like Natasha and want to "work things out" and keep extending invitations. This could be very stressful if you feel swayed by your friend's pressure. You want to leave the friendship, yet your friend is pulling your arm as you walk out the door.

If your friend is pressuring you to talk or provide further explanation, I recommend either not responding or repeating what you have already said. Your friend's plea for more discussion could be their way of trying to talk you out of your decision. Your friend obviously wants your friendship to go back to the way it was. Or, at the very least, your friend wants to deflect blame and responsibility to you. Don't fall for these things. The best response is no response or repeating what you already said in your original message.

Changes in Your Social Life

Your social life could become more difficult if you end your friendship. This depends on how close your former friend is to your other friends.

The first difficulty is not knowing whether to tell your other friends that you have ended this friendship. If your other friends discover you have ended this friendship, then I think it's okay to decline to give the reasons, or if you feel you need to provide some explanation, you can be general. But if your other friends aren't very connected to this friend, then you won't have to say anything to them.

The second difficulty is having to avoid group gatherings this friend might attend. If this is an issue for you, know that it's okay to avoid gatherings where your former friend will be, most especially if you'd be more stressed and overwhelmed than it's worth. What you can do is invite your other friends over so that you are the host and won't have to worry about your former friend being there. You could also focus on getting together with your friends one-on-one or in very small groups where it won't seem strange that your former friend wasn't invited. You could also focus on friends who aren't associated with your former friend.

Your social life may experience some changes, but it won't die.

Guilt

Guilt has been, for me, the biggest challenge of ending a friendship. My guilt was about a few things.

First, I felt guilty about not being able to be what my friend wanted me to be. I love to be a positive, comforting, supportive presence in people's lives. So when I gave and gave then fell flat on my face, empty handed, I felt absolutely terrible. I have sometimes even thought, "This friend would have been better off never knowing me. Now they are more hurt than they were before I came into their lives."

Secondly, I felt guilty for the time I spent *pretending* to be what my friend wanted me to be. By suppressing my true self too often and for too long, I misled my friend about who I really am. I let my friend believe I could be more supportive and giving than I could be.

Thirdly, I felt guilty for not making more effort to work things out, as I explained in chapter 5.

I want to say something here about unhealthy friendships and guilt. Your guilt could be yet another sign that your friend isn't good for you. In unhealthy friendships, you often take more responsibility for your friend than you should;

maybe you feel responsible for your friend's problems, your friend's feelings, your friend's mental health, or your friend's circumstances. If this is the case, then guilt is precisely what your friend *wants* you to feel for letting go of responsibility for them. So, don't fall for it. Letting go of the guilt you feel goes hand in hand with letting go of the responsibility that you were never meant to bear to begin with.

Don't blame yourself for being a finite human being; that's who you're supposed to be. Forgive yourself for any mistakes you made in misleading your friend into thinking you had more to give than you did. Learn from these mistakes and commit to being more authentic in your friendships from this point forward.

Lastly, don't feel bad about being true to yourself for leaving a friendship. Recall the reasons you left the friendship—they're solid and real. You didn't make them up. Don't let guilt tempt you to reach back out to your friend.

I wrestled with this temptation quite a few times before letting it go. I had to remind myself of what I already knew.

You can't fix the feelings your friend has in the aftermath of you leaving the friendship. However, know that being true to yourself was the best outcome possible for both of you. This friendship was a learning experience for your friend as well as for you. All we can each do is live, learn, and do our best going forward.

I hope my book has helped you make the smoothest possible exit from your friendship. I wish both you and your former friend well. I absolutely wish your former friend the ability to grow and learn and form healthy and happy friendships. And I wish you self-forgiveness, a deeper understanding of healthy friendships, and the ability to be more and more yourself each day.

ABOUT THE AUTHOR

Cara Menae Miller has a master's degree in Clinical Counseling. Her favorite subjects are philosophy, religion, and psychology, which she studies for pleasure. She especially loves analyzing people and relationships. In her free time, she enjoys nature walks, rollerblading, cooking, reading, writing, and spending time with friends, family, and children. She's a highly sensitive person and is passionate about lifestyle choices that honor sensitivity. She is also the author of *How to Get Over a Crush on a Friend* and *My HSP Journal: Quotes and writing space for highly sensitive people.*

My book is self-published. If you found it helpful, will you take a minute to let others know by rating and reviewing it on Amazon? Reviews make it possible for my book to be noticed and read by a wider audience. Thank you so much! -Cara

---

[i] Aron, Elaine N. The Highly Sensitive Person. Accessed December 4, 2019. https://hsperson.com/.
[ii] Mello, Anthony De. *The Way to Love: Meditations.* Anand, India: Gujarat Sahitya Prakash, 1995.

[iii] Raypole, Crystal. "Victim Mentality: 16 Signs and Tips to Deal with It." Healthline. Healthline Media, December 12, 2019. https://www.healthline.com/health/victim-mentality.

Printed in Great Britain
by Amazon